IMAGES OF ENGLAND

BIDDULPH
VOLUME II

IMAGES OF ENGLAND

BIDDULPH
VOLUME II

DEREK J. WHEELHOUSE

TEMPUS

Dedicated to the people of Biddulph and in particular all those Bidolfians who have contributed the pictures in this book.

Frontispiece: The gardening class at Biddulph Church School in 1914.

First published 2005

Tempus Publishing Limited
The Mill, Brimscombe Port,
Stroud, Gloucestershire, GL5 2QG
www.tempus-publishing.com

© Derek J. Wheelhouse, 2005

British Library Cataloguing in Publication Data.
A catalogue record for this book is available from the British Library.

ISBN 0 7524 3463 2

Typesetting and origination by Tempus Publishing Limited.
Printed in Great Britain.

Contents

Acknowledgements

I wish to thank the following people for the loan of their postcards and photographs, without which it would not have been possible to publish this book: Mrs Adderley, Mrs J. Booth, Mr J. Chadwick, Mrs A. Chadwick, Mr John Condliffe of the *Congleton Chronicle*, Mrs A. Davis, Mrs M. Fernyhough, Mr J. Garside, Mr A. Green, Mr J. Hancock, Mr A.J. Hargreaves, Mrs C. Heathcote, Mr L. Kirkham, Mr E. Lovatt, Mr G. Lomas, Mr R. Machin, Mr C. McClane, Mr D. Meir, Mrs Mellor, Mrs Ogden, Mrs Owen, Mr H. Page, Mr G. Pass, Mr R. Pill, Mrs Roberts, Mr D. Rogers, Mrs D. Shallcross, Mr R. Shaw, Mr J. Sherratt, Mr W. Sherratt, Mrs A. Stanway, Mrs A. Turnock, Mrs G. Unwin, Mr K. Walton and Mr B. Wright.

Introduction

Following the publication of the first book on Biddulph in 1997, all the material for which was culled from the people I knew or to whom I was referred, an appeal was made through the local newspaper, the *Biddulph Chronicle*, for further material. The response was immediate, but unfortunately the source rapidly dried up and, after two years, only a little more than half the photographs necessary for a second volume had materialised. The breakthrough occurred when the Biddulph librarian, Mrs Irene Turner, posed the question 'Would it be a good idea to resurrect the History Society?' which had ceased to exist through lack of support, many years ago. The new Biddulph & District Historical and Genealogical Society, which held its first meeting in January 2002, has since gone from strength to strength and from this the necessary material for a new book has been found.

The town of Biddulph, which was called Bradley Green up to the 1930s when it changed its name to that of the district, developed from 1860 onwards in response to the increasing workforce required by Robert Heath for his new colliery and ironworks at Black Bull. The first houses built in the lower High Street were basic terraced properties, where the front room was often used for selling provisions. These properties are still occupied by shops and small businesses today. The properties built in the upper High Street from 1900 onwards were still terraced but of better quality and built primarily as shops for the owners, who had more spacious living accommodation behind and above the shop. Today only one shop owner lives on the premises. Since the 1960s, some adjacent properties have been combined and a few areas have been demolished and new properties built on the site.

The one fundamental change to Biddulph since the publication of the previous book is that the long-awaited town relief road has been constructed, which will hopefully lead to the pedestrianisation of the town centre sometime in the future.

As time passes, information is more difficult to uncover and can be lost altogether. In this book there are fewer names on many of the photographs than there were in the previous one. Perhaps this book will prompt memories which will help to fill those gaps. Any such information would be gladly received at the Biddulph library, Staffordshire Moorland.

one

The
Countryside

William Nixon at Hot Lane Farm, Biddulph Moor. He married Sarah Ann Mellor on 16 March 1874 at Christ Church, Biddulph Moor.

A carnival held on Biddulph Moor probably some time in the 1920s. It was known locally as Hospital Saturday and was held to raise money for the North Stafford Infirmary.

A view looking towards Job Wills Rock, above the Hurst and to the south of Troughstone Hill on Biddulph Moor. The Lancaster family lived close by and the name of the rock is said to be derived from Job Lancaster's son William.

The death of Miss Nina Biddulph was announced in the *Biddulph Chronicle* on 25 June 1937. The views in this and the following two photographs on page 12 are taken from the 1937 sale catalogue of Biddulph Old Hall which was auctioned by Maple & Company, London and sold for £1,400.

A photograph of Biddulph Old Hall in 1994, taken after the collapse of part of the west wall following high winds.

Biddulph Old Hall in 1898, looking from the higher ground on the eastern side of the house. It was on this side during the English Civil War that the Parliamentarian cannon 'Roaring Meg' was sited in 1644, causing Mrs Biddulph to prevail upon the other occupants of the house to surrender. This picture was taken before the top of the only remaining pepper-pot tower was blown down during the early hours of one Sunday morning in January 1901.

Mr and Mrs John Close of Biddulph Hall Farm with five of their twelve children. From left to right (with the married names of their daughters given): Mrs Esther Maer, Mrs Ada Davis (of Davis's bicycle shop, Biddulph, see p. 41), Mr John Close, Misses Miriam Campbell and Harriet Wood on the swing, Mrs Close and master John Capstick Close. Mr Close moved to Biddulph in 1886, renting the farm from Mr Stanier, and stayed there until his retirement.

The mill pool of the Hurst silk mill owned in 1840 by the Revd William Henry Holt, the vicar of St Lawrence, Biddulph (and uncle of James Bateman), for whom Elmhurst was built when James moved into the Grange. In 1862 the mill was destroyed by fire and the occupiers' son, Samuel Hathan (Hawthorne) was accused of robbing and setting it alight.

The silk mill owned and occupied by William Stonier in 1840. John Wesley visited Biddulph in 1761 and in a footnote in his journal later written by someone other than Wesley himself it states that 'Wesley's host was Mr William Stonier of The Hurst, Biddulph, chief Trustee of Congleton Chapel, a zealous Local Preacher, a man of wealth'. This picture was taken at the beginning of the twentieth century when it was the home of Thomas Gibson and his wife Jane Sleigh Stonier.

Thomas Gibson and his family at The Hurst, *c.* 1900. From left to right: Annie Gibson, Thomas Gibson, Lily Rose Gibson, Jane Sleigh Gibson(*née* Stonier) and William Stonier Gibson.

Mr James Arthur Lees and his family on the front steps of his garden at Moor House in 1927.

Mill Cottage, probably sometime in the 1920s. It was the home of Thomas Walley, the last miller at Biddulph Mill, and then that of Tom Billinge, a colourful local character.

Opposite below: Biddulph Mill in the early part of the twentieth century. The gentleman is Thomas Walley, a farmer and miller who lived in the adjacent Mill Cottage.

The drive wheel of Biddulph Mill. The lady is thought to be the wife of the miller, Thomas Walley.

Thomas Walley junior, the son of Mr Thomas Walley. The rear of the mill can be seen on the right.

In 1860 James Bateman created a private walk between the Grange and the home of his son, Robert, at Biddulph Old Hall. It crossed the brook running through Gibacre field by a stone bridge bearing the date 1862 (recently restored to its former glory), passing under Fold Lane through a tunnel and then crossing the stream in the Clough by means of a rustic bridge, before continuing on to the Old Hall.

The rustic bridge which at one time crossed the stream which flows down the Clough from the Biddulph Mill pool to join the Biddulph Brook in the valley bottom.

The Grange estate workshop was on the site of what is now the Grange Country Park visitor centre. Timber from the estate was cut up with a saw powered by a water turbine which was supplied with water piped from the lake, created for Robert Heath in 1903. A water turbine has been reinstalled to generate electricity to supply power to the visitor centre and any excess is fed into the National Grid.

This typical one-up, one-down stone cottage was situated close to the junction of Fold Lane and Grange Road at Poolfold. At one time there was a tollgate on the turnpike road at the junction. Before the road ceased to be a turnpike road in 1870, it was the home of the tollgate keeper.

Storm damage in the area of Moorhouse/Elmhurst in the early twentieth century. The man on the right is Mr Thomas Cook.

A tree felled by a whirlwind in 1994 on the land between the Woodhouse School and the National Trust Grange garden. The gardeners, hearing a roaring noise, rushed to see the tree being picked up and then suddenly dropped from a height of ten feet. Its size can be judged from the author's four-year-old granddaughter standing in the foreground.

A dwelling is shown on this site on the Mainwaring estate map of 1597. The Falls denotes a clearing in the woodland that once covered most of the Biddulph valley. The stone house probably dates from the first half of the nineteenth century when James Hall (the coal agent for Hugh Henshall Williamson who owned the nearby Falls colliery and fifty-seven acre estate) was living there in 1834. Falls colliery had ceased working by 1848. In 1851 James Hall was still living there, being described as a farmer. In 1860 it was occupied by Thomas Alcock, farmer and cheese factor.

The White House, situated in Akesmore Lane, is the oldest dwelling in Biddulph. The thatched portion of the property is the best-preserved example of its kind in the Staffordshire Moorlands. Tree-ring dating estimated the felling date of the cruck frame timber to be 1580. Its alternative name 'Holly Lane' gave the name to the best house coal in the North Staffordshire coalfield.

The White House at the very end of the nineteenth century. The lady is Mrs Sarah Hodgkinson, the grandmother of the small boy, who is William Henry Kirkham.

Above: Early in the twentieth century there were still many small thatched cottages in the Gillow Heath area. This one stood in Mow Lane close to the junction with Wedgwood Lane.

Left: Mrs Mary Bailey and her daughter Phyllis at their cottage in Wedgwood Lane, Gillow Heath, Biddulph, *c.* 1908.

Saturday afternoon cricket at Knypersley, when its cricket pavilion appeared to be in its heyday. The affluence of the club was closely bound with its connection to the Biddulph Valley Coal & Ironworks, owned by Robert Heath.

Childerplay Farm stood on the east side of Childerplay Road near to its junction with Bemersley Road. It is on the site of what was once Childerplay colliery, which existed as early as 1775. In 1810 it came under the ownership of James and John Bateman, and the rich coal seams in the area were probably the reason why James purchased the Knypersley estate for his son John. Although Childerplay colliery drew coal up to the time Robert Heath came to Biddulph in 1857, John never exploited the wealth of coal as his father James intended. This picture was taken when the farm was owned by Robert Heath and tenanted by Thomas William Haydon, *c.* 1918. In the centre is Mrs Haydon with her eldest daughter Betsy Elizabeth and youngest son, Joseph Bainbridge. In the background is Childerplay Mission, which stood at the junction of Childerplay and Bemersley Road. The farm was demolished in the 1930s.

Right: Greenway Bank Hall at the beginning of the twentieth century. In 1778 the estate was acquired by Hugh Henshall, James Brindley's brother-in-law, who completed the construction of the Trent & Mersey Canal after James' death. It then passed to his nephew, Hugh Henshall Williamson, who rebuilt the house in 1828 and lived there until his death in 1867. In 1871 Robert Heath paid £19,000 for the mansion and 214 acres. Members of the Heath family lived in the Hall until 1971. In 1973 it was bought by Staffordshire County Council together with 121 acres. The house, which had been vandalised, was demolished and the remainder turned into a country park.

Mr Roland Taylor, tenant farmer at Meadow Stile Farm, Brown Lees, *c.* 1920. During this period the main occupations in the area were that of coal miner, iron worker or agricultural labourer.

Greenway Hall, Knypersley, Biddulph in March 1973, after Staffordshire County Council acquired the house in order to create a country park. It was shortly after this that the house was demolished. (*Congleton/Biddulph Chronicle*)

Hurst Tower was built in 1872 for the Revd William Henry Holt's two sons, who were described in the local directory as sand merchants, extracting and selling sand from the quarry close to their home.

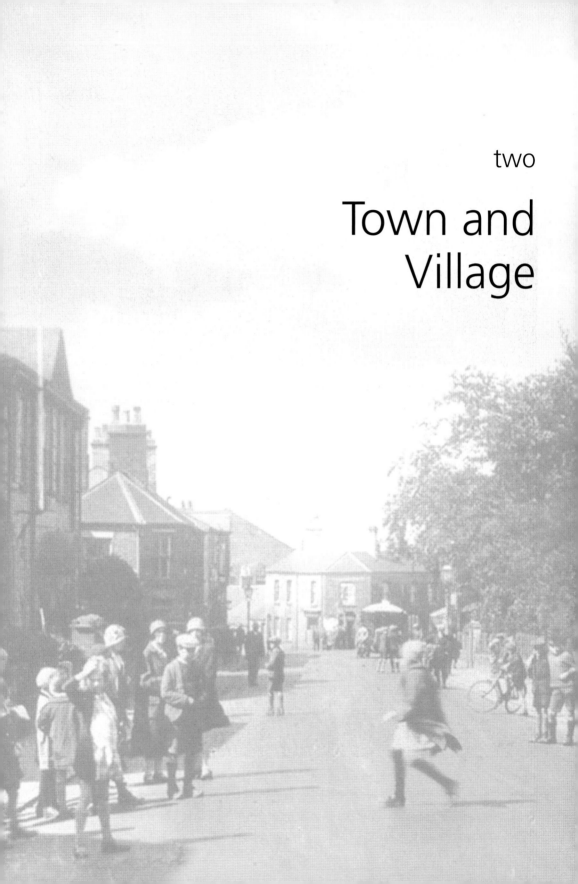

two

Town and Village

The smithy and church, together with the school at Knypersley, were all built by John Bateman around 1850 to serve the community and enhance the area close to his home at Knypersley Hall. The smithy ceased working as such when William Taylor retired in 1947, his family having been blacksmiths there for the previous 100 years.

The opening of the Biddulph relief road/bypass in October 2003. The first small piece of land for a bypass had been acquired by the Council in 1939; local people had been seriously campaigning for its construction since 1965.

A view looking down Biddulph High Street, *c.* 1968. There is little change from earlier days other than the modernisation of the shop fronts and the fact that fewer shop owners lived over and behind their properties. Victor Value, on the right, was one of the first supermarkets in the town, set up in Nos 87 and 89 in 1966 but did not trade for long, closing its doors by 1969.

The High Street, *c.* 1930. The District Bank, on the right at No. 63, was built in 1924. The shop at No. 59 below the bank was Rowley's newsagents and stationers, on this site by 1912. Described in the local directories as a printer, Frederick Rowley was also a photographer producing many local postcards of the area.

The western side of Biddulph High Street looking from its junction with King Street. The District Bank is on the extreme right behind railings. The building on the near side of the left junction with Wharf Road is the Conservative Club, built in 1907, and on the far side is the Public Hall, which was demolished in 1970. The apex roof in the distance is the Primitive Chapel in Station Road, renamed in 1896 having previously been called Chapel Street.

Bradbury's Row was renamed South View in 1896 by the newly created (1894) Biddulph Urban District Council, when they also decided to give numbers to all the properties in the town. The Bradbury family who came to Biddulph from Lancashire in the 1840s developed and owned Bradley Green colliery until Robert Heath took it over in 1887 and closed it in 1894. This row of terraced houses was built in the early 1860s for officials and workers at the colliery.

The east side of Biddulph High Street looking north towards Congleton, *c.* 1960. In the distance is the junction with Station Road, which bears to the left. The tree on the right stands in front of the old Council Offices. Centre right is the junction with King Street and immediately beyond is the District Bank (now the National Westminster) which was built in 1924. Except for the buildings in the far distance the properties were built in the early 1900s.

Biddulph High Street looking south towards Tunstall, *c.* 1960. No. 49, J. W. Bentley's, high-class tobacconist and confectioner, was established by 1928 and No. 51, Harry Machin's ladies and gentlemen's outfitters, by 1936. Neither business exists today. The Union Jack stands in front of the old Council Offices which was replaced in 1966 by the new Town Hall. The building on the extreme right is the Public Hall (demolished in 1970), and immediately beyond is the Conservative Club, built in 1907. In the distance is the top of the High Street and the start of Tunstall Road.

Biddulph High Street on a wet November day in 1981. Rowley's newsagent on the left has been in the same premises since it was first built in the early 1900s, and still trades under the same name today. (*Congleton/Biddulph Chronicle*)

Lower High Street, Biddulph, *c.* 1968. Nos 2 to 34 are on the left. The Swan stands on the right of the Westminster Bank, the substantial frontage of which has now been replaced by a less interesting conventional shop window.

The start of Biddulph High Street looking south from Albert Square, *c.* 1965. No. 1 is on the left and No. 2 on the right. This property was built in the early 1860s in response to the need to accommodate the growing workforce of miners and iron workers employed by Robert Heath at his developing Biddulph Valley Coal & Ironworks. The monument was erected in 1922 in memory of the men from Biddulph killed in the First and subsequently Second World War.

The same view as in the previous photograph, taken forty years later.

Looking (in the opposite direction to the previous picture) down Congleton Road in the 1930s. The Roebuck public house standing on the right was built at about the same time as the lower High Street (1860s) in response to the increasing number of miners and ironworkers coming to work at the colliery and ironworks being developed at Black Bull by Robert Heath.

A little further down Congleton Road than the previous picture. The property on the left existed before 1876, while that on the right was not built until after 1900. The junction on the right leads to Wells Close, where in 1930 Ralph Davis had his motor repair garage (see page 67). The area later became the Wells bus company yard and garage before being acquired by the Potteries Motor Traction Company (PMT) in 1958 (see p. 66).

The Biddulph Arms Hotel situated at the junction of Halls Road and Mow Lane on the left and Smithy Lane on the right, at the same period as the two previous photographs (1930s). The two stone cottages on the right were built in 1877 by Charles Henry Mainwaring of Whitmore Hall. He and his family had owned much of the land on the western side of the valley for many centuries. In 1881 the far cottage was occupied by George Pointon who, together with his family, was a blacksmith at the adjacent smithy up to the time it was demolished.

The Biddulph Arms Hotel at the end of the nineteenth century. It was built in 1874 to replace the ancient Church House Inn sited on the east side of Biddulph church. The Church House was demolished by Robert Heath when he closed the road running close to his recently acquired Grange estate and constructed in its place the Grange Road as it is today. The hotel, when new, was surrounded by land which included a bowling green and other features where the local population could relax after their hard labour in the coal mine and at the ironworks.

Above: The A527 Biddulph to Congleton road looking north from Smithy Lane at the end of the 1960s, shortly after the road had been widened. The land between the edge of the road and the newly built stone wall on the right was bought in 1939 by the Local Authority for a future bypass which finally materialised in 2003.

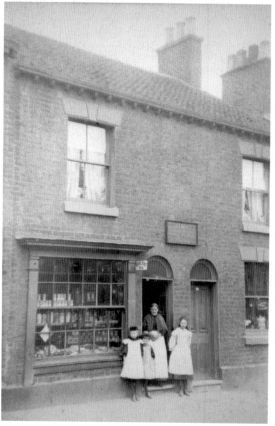

Left: Thomas Sherratt's greengrocer's shop on the south side of the Golden Lion public house in Tunstall Road, *c.* 1900. There had been a greengrocer of that name in Bradley Green since 1876 and by 1921 there was still a Thomas and William Sherratt in both Tunstall Road and the High Street. It was Thomas Sherratt who built the Free Mission Hall in 1886 (adjacent to the Crown and Cushion) for those people who wished to be neither Primitive or Wesleyan Methodists.

Right: William, son of Thomas Sherratt who built the Mission in the High Street in 1886 (see p.38).

Below: Pollard and Butterworth had established their business as dealers in wireless and agents for Singer sewing machines at No. 91 High Street by 1928. It was managed by Mr R. Shaw, seen standing at the door of the shop. In 1957 it was taken over by Mr Derek Wain and in 2004 it still continues in the same line of business, although no longer selling Singer sewing machines.

No. 79 High Street, a confectioners run by the Misses Brandreth between 1912 and 1954. Those who knew and sampled their vanilla slices and sugar buns, baked at the rear of the shop and still warm when put in the paper bag, will never forget their delicious confectionery. There are very few places where you can buy that quality of confectionery today.

By 1912 and until after 1940, John Higgins was a bootmaker at No. 65 High Street, on the corner of Kings Street where Barclays Bank now stands. There was always a requirement for several boot- and clog-makers in the town to cater for the workmen's needs, up to 1928 when the ironworks closed, and then onwards for the colliery.

Mr Ralph Davis was established as a bicycle dealer at No. 14 in the High Street as early as 1912. Mrs Ada Davis, his wife, is seen here together with her son Norman, aged seventeen, at the door of their shop in 1932.

Gordan Evans' sweetshop at No. 9 High Street, Biddulph, *c.* 1952.

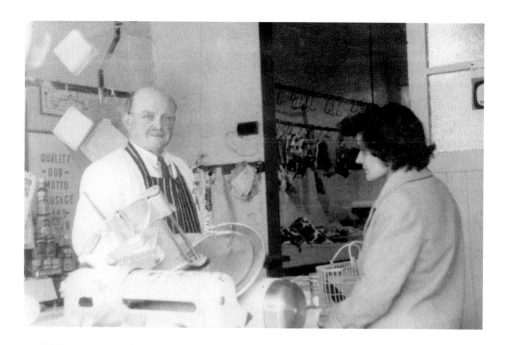

Above: Mr John Clowes, a butcher, at his shop at No. 13 High Street in the 1960s. James Simpson, also a butcher, had occupied the property as early as 1884, followed by Jess Simpson until 1944 when it was bought by Mr Clowes. Since 1982 his son Robert has continued to run the family business, the property having been a butcher's shop for at least 120 years.

Left: Frederick Booth was a fishmonger and fruiterer at No. 2 High Street in 1928 and continued in the same trade at the premises until at least 1940.

Ebenezer Whalley's shop at No. 6 Albert Square, Biddulph, in the early twentieth century. Ebenezer worked at Brown Lees colliery and on one occasion, when he injured his foot, two men wheeled him to Albert Square in a wheelbarrow where he said that he could walk the rest of the way to his home in Albert Street. From left to right: his eldest daughter Martha, Edith, Ada, his wife Martha, and Ebenezer.

Ebenezer Whalley with his ice cream cart in Station Road. The old cottages in the background were demolished more than ten years ago to make way for the Biddulph bypass, which was completed in 2003.

Having established his business in 1856, William Garside was first mentioned in *Kelly's Directory* of 1872 as a furniture dealer. It was not until 1892 that he was described as a furniture dealer and undertaker in Cross Street. The business still exists today on the same site, carrying out exactly the same services to the people of Biddulph as it did over 110 years ago.

The 'Homestead', John Street, built around 1910 as a home and surgery by Dr James Craig, physician, surgeon and medical officer for the Biddulph district. He retired in the early 1930s and was succeeded as medical officer by Dr T.C. Murphy, while Dr Gibson Miller took up residence in the Homestead. It continued as a surgery until the late 1960s when a new medical centre was opened.

Barbers Picture Palace, Kings Street, just across the road from the Homestead, was opened in 1910 by Dr Craig. It was the second picture house opened by Mr G.H. Barber after the one in Tunstall in 1909. These two were the first of many he was to build in the Potteries and further afield. Barbers eventually became Crookes Picture Palace and finally closed in the 1950s.

Two cottages and land on the site of the present Town Hall, which was acquired by the Urban District Council in 1937 with the intention of demolishing the buildings and erecting new Council Offices. In 1941 the larger cottage was converted into offices for the Town Clerk and other officers and in 1946 the prefabricated building was erected to house all the other council departments. Previous to 1941, council business was carried out in what was formerly the Odd Fellows Hall, built in 1856 and purchased from them in 1895 to become known locally as the Public Hall.

Left: These buildings continued to be used by the Town Clerk and all district officers and staff until 1964, when they were demolished to make way for the new Town Hall.

Below: Biddulph Town Hall, completed in 1966, was officially opened on 10 May that year by Chairman of the Council, Cllr Len Jackson JP. During the time of building, the administrative duties of the Council were conducted in the gymnasium in Wharf Road, opposite the Public Hall.

Opposite below: Demolition of the Public Hall and shops in November 1970 in preparation for the first major commercial development in Biddulph since the building of the Congleton Co-operative store in 1898. Originally built in 1856 for the Odd Fellows Society, it was acquired in 1895 by the newly formed Urban District Council. (*Congleton/Biddulph Chronicle*)

Biddulph's new county branch library, costing £8,400, opened in October 1965, the first permanent library the town had had for many years. In the 1950s the library stood behind the Public Hall. It was then moved for a short time into Nos 14 and 16 John Street before being rehoused in a prefabricated structure behind the old Council Offices. Larger than its previous accommodation, the new library housed 16,000 books. Classical and jazz records were also available, but no pop records. Its membership was 3,549 including 1,300   children. The Branch Librarian was Mr Ransley. (*Congleton/Biddulph Chronicle*)

Construction being carried out on the site of the old Public Hall in September 1971, to create four shops with living accommodation and the first purpose-built supermarket to be built in Biddulph. (*Congleton/Biddulph Chronicle*)

Biddulph's first real supermarket, Key Markets, opened at No. 36 High Street, on 25 August 1972. (*Congleton/Biddulph Chronicle*)

A further major development took place in 1985 with the opening of the new United Co-op store, which replaced the shops of the Congleton Equitable and Industrial Society built in 1898. The older stores included drapery, boot, clothing, furnishing and butchery departments housed in a building that many found much more architecturally pleasing than that of the present-day modern store. (*Congleton/Biddulph Chronicle*)

In 1986 the Co-op pharmacy department occupied the old property which, between 1924 and 1940, had been the chemist shop belonging to Jabez Oakes and which has since been redeveloped by Wetherspoons. Shortly after this, the pharmacy department was relocated to where the for sale sign can be seen on the property below and adjacent to the new store. (*Congleton/Biddulph Chronicle*)

The closing-down sale of Woolworths in June 1986. It was the first national store to establish itself in Biddulph High Street and was opened in September 1957. By 1986 Biddulph had lost its main sources of local employment in coal mining and heavy engineering and was becoming more of a commuter town, with people working outside the area and taking their custom elsewhere. (*Congleton/Biddulph Chronicle*)

Biddulph Moor in the late 1960s at the junction of Woodhouse Lane, Hot Lane, Wraggs Lane and New Street. The old gentleman walking from his stone cottage at the junction of Four Lane Ends up to his local shop is Bill Finney, one of the last truly genuine Biddulph Moor characters. Although Bill's stone cottage has since been replaced by a modern house, the village shop still serves the village.

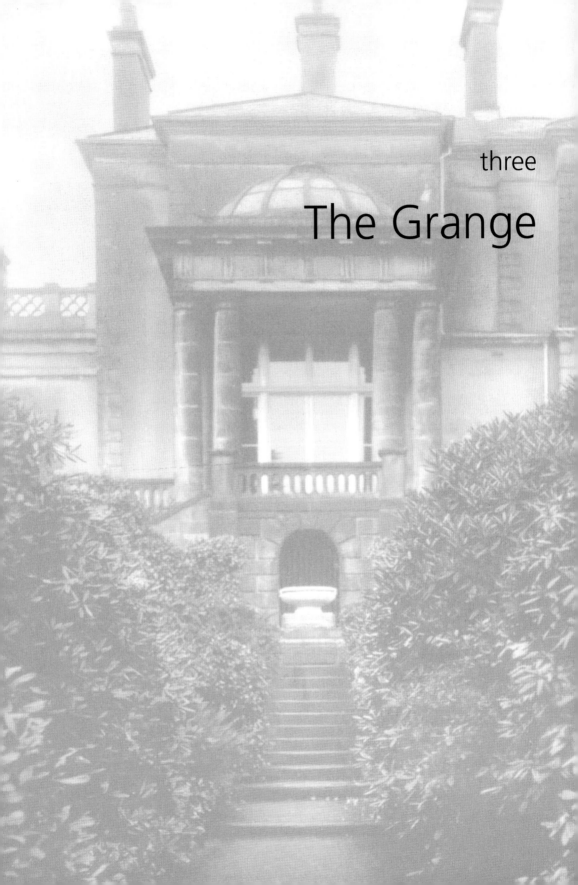

three

The Grange

Right: The Grange Lodge, sadly vandalised, standing at the end of Lime Avenue between the Grange house and the parish church of St Lawrence. Demolished some time during the early 1960s, it was last occupied by William Shufflebotham (one of Robert Heath's gardeners) who was appointed as head gardener for the hospital in 1923 and remained as such until he retired in 1945.

Below: Luke Pointon, a young under-gardener in 1861 to James Bateman, was to become head gardener to both Robert Heaths. His pocket diary for 1898 has survived and in it on 19 January he records that he 'moved a large Chestnut in the Avenue'. The photograph shows Luke supervising the moving of a large tree, an operation which normally would take three days to complete: one day to lift, one to move and one to replant it.

Opposite above: Luke Pointon (holding the reins), head gardener to Robert Heath, at the front of his house, which together with his nursery stood on the opposite side of the road to St Lawrence church. The house was demolished in the early 1960s to make way for the development of the new houses that now stand on the site.

Opposite below: A photograph of Pointons Nursery taken by the *Daily Herald* in 1936.

Luke Pointon and his family in the garden of his home The Nurseries, Congleton Road, which was opposite St Lawrence church.

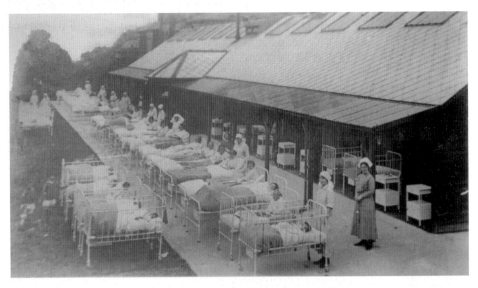

In 1923 Robert Heath handed over the Grange house and estate (where he and his family had lived since 1874) to the Staffordshire Orthopaedic Hospital. The wooden wards were built on its cherry orchard and the hospital was officially opened by HRH the Prince of Wales on 14 June 1924. Two years later the hospital trustees stated that they were financially unable to keep the hospital open. In 1926 it was bought by Lancashire County Council for £10,000, for the care and education of the crippled children of east Lancashire.

Right: The Grange garden and house after it was rebuilt, following the fire in 1896 and before the establishment of the hospital. The Dahlia Walk on the left was filled in to make way for the erection of the wooden wards on the cherry orchard in 1923. The view is taken from the Shelter House which was also demolished but subsequently restored by the National Trust, who acquired the garden in 1988, opening it to the public in 1991. The view is exactly the same today.

Below: Looking east along the terrace in front of the Grange. The room over the tunnel was Mrs Maria Bateman's boudoir, a part of the house that was not affected by the fire in 1896. At one time it was used by the hospital matron as an office and today it forms part of one of the nine apartments that have been created within the house. The hospital wards once stood on the right behind the boudoir.

BIDDULPH GRANGE ORTHOPAEDIC HOSPITAL
ROWLEYS SERIES.

Top left: The west end of the Grange looking north along the Italian garden towards the house. This part of the original Bateman house was little affected in the 1896 fire and was retained by Robert Heath in his rebuild, except for the addition of the portico. Visitors to the National Trust property first pass along this path to enter this unique early Victorian garden created by James Bateman in the period around 1841 to 1869.

Top right: The north side of the Grange house following the disastrous fire in 1896. The glass houses and conservatories, part of James Bateman's original house, were removed and not replaced when Robert Heath rebuilt the property.

Bottom: This charming picture of Biddulph May Day celebrations was taken in 1922 just before Robert Heath gave the Grange house and estate to the Staffordshire Orthopaedic Hospital in 1923. It is being held on land which is part of Woodhouse Farm. Behind the festivities is the boundary ha-ha wall of Mr Heath's tennis court and the Grange gardens.

four

Transport

Like everywhere else in the country, the horse and cart was the earliest form of bulk transport in the Biddulph valley. Although this scene was taken at the turn of the twentieth century, this mode of transport was still in use until motor transport began to replace it from the 1920s onwards. Even so, its use for local carriage only disappeared completely by the 1960s.

Early coal mining brought the railed tramway to the area, for which horses were the motive power. The Falls rail-road was constructed in 1809 by Hugh Henshall Williamson to carry coal from the Falls collieries up to a wharf on Congleton Road overlooking the Cheshire Plain. The rails, which were L-shaped and four feet in length, were laid on stone-block sleepers. The site of the Falls colliery is to the right, just off the edge of the photograph (taken in 1972). These few remaining sleepers lead to the site of the Lower Falls colliery where there were two shafts close to the Railway Cottages that are on the far left of the picture.

Left: The Falls colliery rail-road stone-block sleepers looking towards the west, leading to the coal wharf on Congleton Road 300 vertical feet above. The rail-road was two-thirds of a mile long at an average gradient of 1 in 10, so the wagons can only have been small to enable a horse to pull one up the steep slope.

Below: The Biddulph Valley Branch of the North Staffordshire Railway (NSR), looking from the bridge at Brindley Ford adjacent to the old Black Bull towards Victoria colliery, formerly the Biddulph Valley Coal & Ironworks of Robert Heath. The branch was built principally to serve the collieries along its route. The NSR, affectionately known locally as the 'Knotty', operated a limited passenger service along this line between 1864 and 1927.

The Biddulph Valley Branch Railway approaching the site of Biddulph station, *c.* 1960. The Railway Cottages on the right, which once housed railway employees, were demolished soon after 1970.

A little further north of the Railway Cottages. On the right is the old platform and goods shed and on the left is the stationmaster's house standing alongside the Station Road level crossing.

Although the railway was closed to passenger traffic in 1927, holiday and school specials continued to be run over the branch line up to the end of the 1960s. This one is standing in front of the old goods shed at Biddulph station on the up line to Stoke in 1957.

This and the following two photographs were taken in 1954 when the train taking coal from Victoria colliery to Brunswick Wharf, Congleton, became derailed at Horton's crossing at Lea Forge and the engine plunged down the embankment. Miraculously, neither the driver or the fireman were badly injured.

Above and left: The train derailment at Horton's crossing at Lea Forge in 1954.

Robert Heath built many of his own locomotives at his Biddulph Ironworks. No. 11, seen here in the sidings on the north side of Brown Lees Road in 1961, was built by Black, Hawthorne of Gateshead, Durham in 1888. It was rebuilt by Robert Heath in 1902 and 1914 and again in 1932 by Cowlishaw Walker. It was originally a Norton colliery engine but by 1953 it had been transferred to Victoria colliery, from where it took coal to the Birchenwood Gas & Coke Co., Kidsgrove, until it was scrapped in 1965.

The important nature of this occasion is not definitely known, but it is possible the photograph was taken in 1924 when HRH the Prince of Wales visited Biddulph to open the Staffordshire Orthopaedic Hospital at the Grange.

Possibly the same occasion as the previous picture. The bus is standing in Wharf Road outside the Public Hall, bought in 1895 by the newly formed Urban District Council.

A bus belonging to Mr Arthur Findlow of the Bird in Hand, Station Road, whose garage was in Cross Street. Bookings for tours were made at No. 2 High Street, his sister's home, from where the vehicles departed. Later departures were made from Findlow's house at No. 1 South View where his sister, Mrs A. Parkinson, took bookings.

Wells Motor Services standing in Tower Square, Tunstall, awaiting departure to Biddulph, sometime in the late 1940s. Earnest Wells commenced operations from No. 4 High Street, Biddulph, in 1914 and continued until 1953 when he was bought out by the Potteries Motor Traction Company (PMT).

The North Western Road Car Company, formed at Macclesfield, ran on the Biddulph to Congleton route in the 1920s. In 1936 they acquired Biddulph and District Motors Ltd, sited at Well Street Garage (where the present library stands) which they occupied until 1961. From then on the fleet was housed in the new garage in Walley Street.

When the PMT acquired Wells in 1953, it was run as a subsidiary until 1958 when it was absorbed into the main company. This gave the PMT its first depot in central Biddulph, in Congleton Road. In 1961 this became insufficient and they moved into the newly built Walley Street Garage along with the North Western, both companies having become part of the British Electric Traction Company in 1942.

The mode of transport of the affluent before the days of the car. The person is probably Mr Leonard Arrowsmith at his home 'Laneside', in Park Lane, Knypersley.

Mr Frank Davis, brother of Mr Ralph Davis, who helped to run a taxi service. The car is one that may have once belonged to Dr T.C. Murphy. One of Frank Davis's tasks was to see that the doctor's car started first thing every morning.

Mr Ralph Davis of No. 14 High Street, at his workshop sited where Wells Close is today. Kelly's 1932 Directory describes his business as Davis & Son, Cycle Agents and Auto Engineers. The cycle shop still exists in 2004 at Nos 20 & 22 on the High Street, Biddulph, run by his daughter-in-law and her son.

Above: During the inter-war years, there was a good living to be made by transporting coal from the local collieries and stone and sand from the surrounding quarries. The photograph suggests that Mr V. Bailey of Gillow Heath is receiving delivery of a new Albion tipper lorry at his local agents.

Left: Mr Samuel Moss, coal merchant and haulage contractor, on the left, collecting coal from Hart's footrail in Woodhouse Lane in the 1930s.

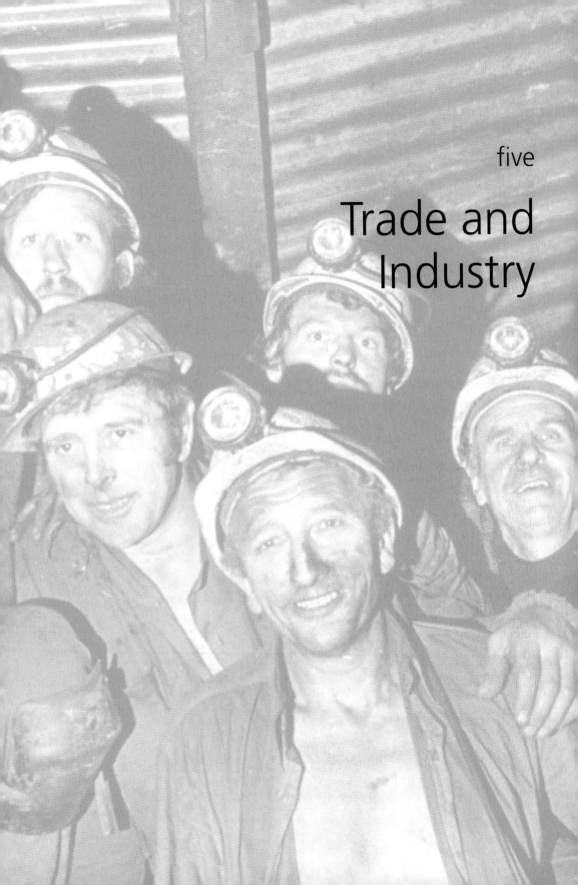

five

Trade and Industry

Left: Robert Heath's Biddulph Valley Ironworks amalgamated with that of Lowmoor of Bradford in 1919 and in 1928 the company went into liquidation. The Biddulph Ironworks had never produced anything other than wrought iron, the demand for which was greatly reduced, it having been replaced by steel. The shell of the blast furnaces stood until 1935, when they were finally demolished.

Below: In the late 1980s and early 1990s the shallow coal that remained unworked at the site of and to the west of Victoria colliery was extracted by opencast working, uncovering the base of the old blast furnaces.

Above: A bell pit exposed at Brindley Ford during the extraction of coal on an area of industrial waste prior to it being landscaped. During the period 1860–1928, the iron slag from Robert Heath's Biddulph Valley Ironworks was tipped over this ground. A bell pit is so named because the coal is extracted from around the bottom of a shallow shaft, before its imminent collapse and abandonment creates the shape of a bell. The Brindley Ford bell pit probably dates from any time between the late sixteenth and early seventeenth century.

Right: A group of colliers at what was probably one of the numerous small coal workings that could be found in the early years of the twentieth century, retrieving the shallow coal left from earlier times. The pit headgear appears to be more substantial than that which would be used during periods of strike.

Coal outcrop working, possibly during the 1926 strike and probably somewhere in the area of Akesmore Lane, Biddulph. At the rear is Tom Price and, from left to right: 'Spraky' Walley, 'Maunch' Whitehurst, Tom Brereton and Frank 'Patch' Cottrell. The latter's granddaughter, Mrs J. Bradbury, only knew of some of these men by their nicknames, which were very common amongst the mining fraternity.

The 1843 Tower Hill colliery building in 1969. Contrary to many printed accounts, this did not house the winding engine, but was the colliery workshops and stores. These included the blacksmiths, saddlery and carpenters shops. The shafts and winding engine were situated at and around the area from which the picture was taken.

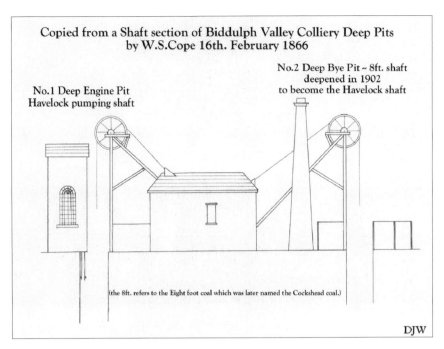

Copied from a Shaft section of Biddulph Valley Colliery Deep Pits by W.S.Cope 16th. February 1866

No.2 Deep Bye Pit ~ 8ft. shaft
deepened in 1902
to become the Havelock shaft

No.1 Deep Engine Pit
Havelock pumping shaft

(the 8ft. refers to the Eight foot coal which was later named the Cockshead coal.)

DJW

No pictures of the pit headgear at Robert Heath's Biddulph Valley colliery have yet been found. This stylised drawing taken from an old shaft section of the colliery provides some idea of how they would have looked.

A view taken from the top of the Victoria shaft headgear. The empty railway sidings suggest that it was taken during the August summer holiday when maintenance would be carried out. The colliery offices are in the left foreground and the electrical power house is behind and to the right.

Colliers underground at Victoria colliery, September 1978. From left to right, back row: Geoff Hartshorne, Peter Evans, Les Taylor, Fred ?, Don Sherratt, Herbert Morris. Front row: Dennis Adderley, Cedric Pass and Frank Myott.

Opposite above: Victoria colliery in 1972 as viewed from its dirt tip. The Victoria shaft headgear are in the centre and those of the Havelock shaft are on the left.

Opposite below: A new Markham steam winding engine was installed at the Victoria shaft in August 1938 to replace the Daglish winder installed in 1898 at the time of the shaft deepening. The engine was installed during the holiday fortnight by Mr Bert Beardmore, the colliery engineer (on the left), together with a team of men.

Opposite above: The Victoria shaft headgear on 24 October 1983 prior to its demolition. Coal was last wound up the shaft in July 1982. The steel headgear was erected in 1925, replacing the original wooden one in use since 1898, when the Magpie shaft was deepened and renamed following the death of Queen Victoria in 1901.

Opposite below: The end of an era. The Victoria shaft headgear immediately after demolition.

Right: The author talking to Vicky Walker of Radio Stoke shortly after the demolition of the Victoria shaft headgear.

Below: Opencast working on the site and to the west of the Victoria colliery from 1986 to 1994. The coal running top right to bottom left is the Bellringer seam or Stoney Eight Feet, so called because of the hard band of sandstone dividing the top and bottom coals. In the foreground is the brick lining of old No. 6 shaft.

Holcombe House in 1929. The home of Mr Thomas Greenhalgh, it was built in 1902 at the junction of Congleton and Mow Lane. The lady on the left is Thomas's wife, Mrs Kitty Greenhalgh (the daughter of Luke Pointon), with their eldest daughter Beatrice.

Opposite above: This photograph shows the inclination of the floor of the worked-out Hams coal seam at Brown Lees opencast site. In the far wall, lighter in colour, are glacial channels which continue on to the line of the Serpentine reservoir. These channels were formed by the melting ice as the glaciers retreated north, as the weather became warmer 12,000 years ago.

Opposite below: The Albion Fustian Mill, Station Road, Biddulph. The person standing by the grindstone is Mr John Brennan, the mill foreman. Behind is Mr Thomas Taylor, Director of the United Velvet Cutters Association and at the rear is Mr Thomas Greenhalgh, manager for the Biddulph area of the United Velvet Cutters Association.

The Old Smithy, Knypersley. Alf Brough, Joe Stoddard and Cyril Gibson are seen here making concrete blocks in the 1950s.

Opposite above: Workers at Jackson's fustian mill on Biddulph Moor in the early years of the twentieth century.

Opposite below: The smithy at Red Cross, Knypersley, built around 1850 by John Bateman of Knypersley Hall on the site of an earlier one. It was regrettably demolished in 1967 to make way for a garage forecourt.

Hurst sand quarry workers, *c.* 1900. Janet Booth's great grandfather is third from the left in the middle row. Many of the men are named Bailey or Gibson.

Lee Forge Colour Works workforce, *c.* 1917. Mr Shadrach Gibson, Surveyor to Biddulph District Council, seated on the right, bought the Lee Forge estate from the executors of Samuel F. Gosling in 1913, first leasing it to Mr Hampton Beckett before selling it to him in March 1918. Beckett then sold it on to his company six months later. The workforce was brought in from their Manchester site and included, from left to right, front row: Mr Henry Wright, works manager, Mr Beckett (bowler hat), to his left Mr Norman Ashton, the chemist responsible for the colour process that produced the cobalt dye. Mr Albert Prince, works engineer, is in the back row fifth from the left.

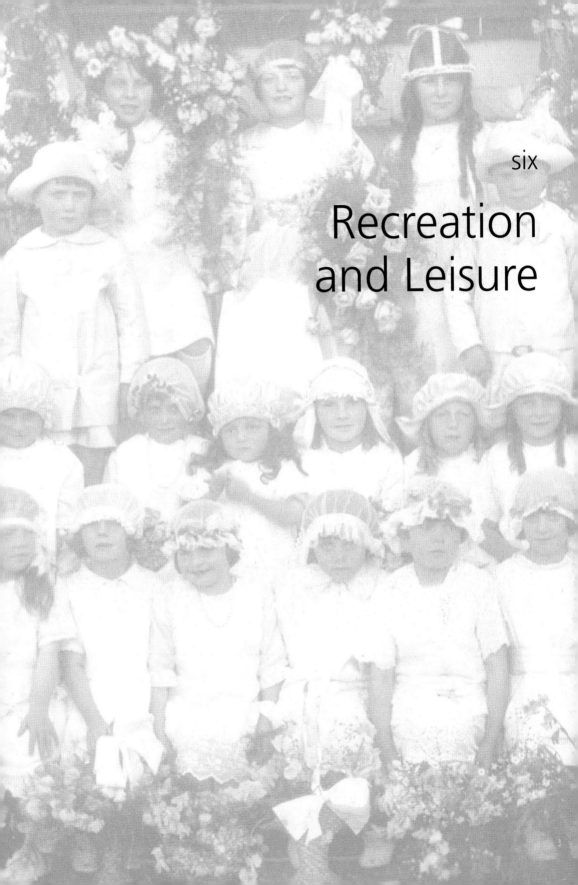

six

Recreation and Leisure

The Gillow Heath Working Men's Club Institute Ltd stood on the opposite side of the road to the 'Staffordshire Knot', Gillow Heath, from about 1922 to 1940. It was closed shortly after Mr Harry Brough became landlord at the Staffordshire Knot public house.

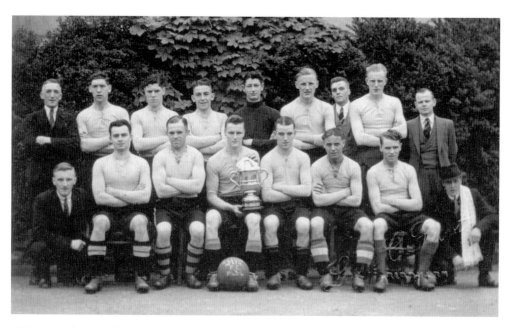

Gillow Heath Football Club 1943/44. From left to right, back row: Albert Vickers, ? Hall, Lenny Lancaster, Billy Fay, Fred Campbell, Arthur Wooley, William Caddy, Jack Wooley, Harold Fitzgerald. Front row: Matt Goodwin, Reg Hilditch, Jim Holland, Alec Hancock, Teddy Holdcroft, Harold Darlington, Tommy Hayden, George Worth (trainer).

The football team brought together in April 1945 by Len Sargeant of the 'Knot' public house, Gillow Heath, to play a charity match against the team of Jock Willcock of the Royal Oak, Biddulph. Eric Bradbury, the owner of the mill at the rear of the Knot, kicked off. From left to right, back row: Bill Shaw, Jack Horton, Tom Hartshorn, Sam Hartshorn, Horace Norwood, Bill Caddy. Front row: Arthur Armitt, Bert Pass, Eric Bradbury, Bert Rhodes, Norman Bailey, Wilf Brough. George Worth is on the left and the bystander is Tom Squires.

Biddulph Moor Welfare Hall. At left rear is Mr Colin Machin. Third from the left in the front row is Mr Herbert Maskery, manager of the Victoria colliery, and the sixth person from the left with the cigarette and wearing the trilby is Mr Shadrach Gibson, engineer to Biddulph Urban District Council.

The Staffordshire Knot, *c.* 1938. From left to right, back row: George Allen, Sam Hartshorne, Tom Plimmer, Jack Ryles, Lizzie Heaps, William Caddy, Millie Sargeant (Brough), Len Sargeant, Gladys Davis (Brammer), Mr Simcock, Dick Whalley, Frank Durber, Bill Davis. Front row: Mr Mitchell, Mr Whalley, Mr Brough, Mr Nixon, Mr Bailey, Charles Lancaster (Doddy), Charlie Hancock, Jack Barlow, Harry Brough (publican).

Opposite above: Members of the first motorcycling club in Biddulph, in Wharf Road in 1913. The motorcyclists and the machines they rode are, from left to right: Messrs Jabez Oakes, chemist (on his NSU), Archie Birchenhall, ironmonger (Aerial), Jim Stoddard, draper (Triumph), Ebenezer and Fred Machin, bakers (Triumphs), Alfred Butterworth, chemist, Mark Stoddard, Co-operative grocer (Singer), and Frank Davis, cycle shop owner (De Dion), with Fred Frost, grocer, holding the machine of Arthur Goodall, manager of the Biddulph Picture Palace (Minerva), while Mr Goodall takes the picture.

Opposite below: Annual visit to the TT Races, Isle of Man, in the 1950s. Organised by Mr J.W. Clowes (butcher), a group of enthusiasts annually made the trip to the Isle of Man, leaving Liverpool on the midnight ferry on Sunday, watching the racing at the same spot (Kate's Cottage) every year and returning home on Monday morning. From left to right, back row: W. Shuffelbottom, D. Sherratt, D. Jennion, A. Gibson. Front row: J. Brammer, J.W. Clowes, W.G. Gibson, -?-.

Cowlishaw Walker outing to Blackpool 1954/55. Front table, from left to right: Arthur Smith, Arthur Foden, Stan Gregory, Bill Williams, Gerald Pass and Cliff Jones.

A rather battered photograph of the officials and committee of Biddulph Band Club 1947/48. From left to right, back row: E. Dale, R. Spencer, J. Shallcross, J. Bossons, H. Sutton, J. Caddy, H. Caddy. Seated: H. Sherratt (trustee), W. Cope (president), S. Copeland (secretary), W. Lowe (vice-president) and G. Bentley.

The 'Black and White Concert Party', *c.* 1947. From left to right: Wilson Mould, Marilyn Cooke, Fred Nixon of Congleton, Lilian Perks (later to become Mrs L.C. Frost) and Tom Bennison. The pianist was Mr Brown of Mossley. Mr Tom Bennison became the chairman of Biddulph Urban District Council in 1952/54 and Mr L.C. Frost in 1956/58.

The Biddulph branch of the British Legion at the Public Hall in 1937/38. The lady in the centre in the white hat is Mrs Sarah Linney, the chairperson of Biddulph District Council in that year. The lady sixth from the left behind the table is Mrs G. Page and standing on her right is Mr Robinson, the School Attendance Officer. The gentleman at the extreme bottom right is Mr H.J. Page. Also in the picture are Mr and Mrs Leese, Mr and Mrs Hargreaves, Mr G. Shaw and Miss Frances Cottrell, teacher at the Biddulph North School.

The dinner given for the employees of the North Western Bus Company in 1960, prior to its moving into the newly built Walley Street Garage in 1961, together with the Potteries Motor Traction Co.

Biddulph Moor Carnival held at Knalow Farm in the late 1920s.

seven

Schools

Biddulph North Council School, *c*. 1930. It was built in 1874, the year that Robert Heath came to live at the Grange. It was a replacement for the small Parish Free School for twelve pupils, built around 1785 and situated at Crabtree Green, now part of the grounds of the National Trust Grange garden.

Children at St Lawrence Church School in 1908, together with the master of the school, Mr George Lawton.

Biddulph North Council School in 1924.

St Lawrence Church School, now Biddulph North Council School, in 1924, just prior to the time when Mr George Lawton (extreme left) was appointed as the headmaster of Knypersley Council School. Mr William Shuttleworth, on the right, replaced him as headmaster.

St Lawrence Church School, *c.* 1932. From left to right: Annie Stanway, Hilda Harrop, Hilda Poole, Emily Beech, Sissie Wheldon, Ethel Barber, Hilda Fitton, Evelyn Stanway, Cissy House, Doris Brown, Doris Pimlott, Betsy Barker, Marie Clowes, Irene Lancaster, Elizabeth Winterton, Annie Alcock, Ena Pickford, Gladys House, Edith Moss. The teacher is Miss Cottrell.

Opposite: The gardening class at Biddulph Church School in 1914.

Sports Day at Biddulph North School, *c.*1950. From left to right, back row: Enid Gibson, Ruth Mayer, Cynthia Grimwood, Shirley Booth, Shirley Goldstraw, Beatrice Stanway. Front row: June Bailey, Hazel Irene Winterton, Iris Edwards, Barbara Heaps.

Above: Pupils at Biddulph Moor Council School in 1909, shortly after the school had been built. The headmaster is Mr H.W. Reeves. From left to right, front row, fourth along ? Copeland, fifth William Proctor, sixth W. Gregory, seventh Len Brown, eighth E. Gibson, ninth A. Gibson, eleventh J. Nixon, twelfth Ernest Mayer.

Right: Herbert William Reeves was master of the National School, Biddulph Moor, in 1892. A new council school was opened in 1909 of which Mr Reeves was still the headmaster in 1921.

Above and below: Two class photographs of pupils at Biddulph Moor Council School in 1921.

Class at Biddulph Moor Church School in 1927. From left to right, back row: William Wilshaw, William Brown, William Mayer, Bert Simms, Arthur Brown, Reg Chaddock, George Wilson, Gordon Bailey, Karl Lancaster. Third row: Lilley Massey, Lena Brown, Dorothy Salmons, Jane Nixon, Annie May Gibson, Muriel Bailey, Millicent Smith, Hilda Beech, Jenny Bailey, Minda Taplin, Freda Shufflebottom. Second row: Frank Machin, Arthur Bailey, Alice Beech, Sarah Lightfoot, ? Goldstraw, Hilda Corishley, Elsie Beech, Hilda Smith, Thomas Biddulph, Vincent Wrench. Front row: Howard Warrender, James Beech, Reg Lovatt, William Bailey, Percy Hulme, Victor Clews.

A fine example of the type of partitioned classroom to be found in most schools in the 1920-50 period before new post-war schools were built. This one is at Biddulph Moor.

Biddulph Moor School, 1949. From left to right, back row: Gerald Pass, Harry Blood, Cecil Watson, Frank Beech, Terry Machin, Graham Bradbury, Joe Stonier, Jack Bailey. Front row: Peter Stanway, George Shufflebottom, Brian Nixon, Frank Stanway, Cyril Brown.

Biddulph Moor Mixed School, 1949. From left to right, back row: Ken Gaskhill, Gordon Ault, George Holdcroft, Derek Cartlidge, Harry Blood, Gerald Pass, Hilary Bould, Frank Beech, Edward Proctor, Bill Bailey. Third row: Mary Mellor, Mary Warren, John Mellor, Cecil Watson, Graham Bradbury, Joe Stonier, Eric Bailey, Mary Bailey, Jean Stonier, Mr Devine. Second row: Edmond Shufflebottom, Jack Bailey, Shirley Burton, Beryl Proctor, Kathleen Page, Hilda Hall, Audrey Proctor, Alma Wilshaw, Hazel Beech, Derek Brown, Peter Stanway. Front row: Frank Stanway, Peter Stanway, Freda Dale, Mabel Bailey, Ann Worthington, Edith Bailey, Edith Gibson, Pamela Bradbury, Hilda Gibson, Bob Plant, George Shufflebottom.

Biddulph Moor School, c. 1949. Standing, back row: -?-, -?-, Harry Blood, Norman Chaddock, teacher Cyril Watson,-?-, Graham Bradbury, Joe Stonier, Jack Bailey, Colin Lancaster. Middle row: Gerald Pass, -?-, George Shufflebottom, Brian Nixon, Terry Machin, Malcolm Doorbar, -?-, -?-. Front row: Peter Stanway, Derek Cartlidge, Bob Plant, Brian Stanway, -?-, -?-, Frank Stanway, Cyril Brown.

Kingsfield School class photograph, 1959. Frank Davis is in the third row on the right, aged six, and Mr Wilfred Hunt is the headmaster.

Knypersley School had been built along with the church, parsonage and smithy for John Bateman of Knypersley Hall at Red Cross crossroads by 1849. They were all built from the local sandstone and they remain (except for the smithy), together with Biddulph church and Biddulph Old Hall, the most impressive old buildings in the area today.

Knypersley Council School in 1933. Mr George Lawton, the headmaster, is on the right. Mr Quinton – in the centre –was later to become the headmaster of Hanley High School.

Knypersley Junior School, *c.* 1949. From left to right, back row: Eileen Hollis, Marion Doorbar, Jean Gibson, Jean Caddy, Beryl Cook, Marie Boon, Sheila Harrison. Middle row: Marie Copeland, Joan Fradley, Pauline Ault, Sylvia Whalley, Hilda Mould. Front row: Sylvia Johnson, Sheila Sanderson, Jean Copeland, Sheila Bennison, Sheila Gibson.

Knypersley Junior School, *c.* 1948. From left to right, back row: Marion Doorbar, Eileen Hollis, Sheila Sanderson, Philip Goodwin, -?-, Jean Gibson, Doreen Lowe, John Fower, Beryl Cook, Jean Caddy. Standing next to back row: Colin Bloor, Bill Brereton, Marie Boon, Sheila Harrison, Hilda Mould. Sitting, middle row: teacher Mr O'Mara, Joan Fradley, Marie Copeland, Sylvia Whalley, Kenneth Kirkham. Standing: Sheila Bennison. Sitting, front row: Alan Sargeant, Geoff Gidman, Alan Shallcross, Dennis Dale, Eric Pointon, Eric Knight, Barry Leslie, Barry Harrison, Pauline Ault, Jean Copeland, Sheila Gibson, Sylvia Johnson.

Knypersley Church Football Club, 1916–1917.

Biddulph Moor football team playing in plain shirts at Knypersley cricket ground in the early 1960s. The team secretary, George Pass, is standing behind the goal wearing a flat cap.

eight

Local Events

Albert Square, Biddulph, 12 June 1924. Crowds awaiting the arrival of HRH the Prince of Wales on his way to officially open the Staffordshire Orthopaedic Hospital at the Grange.

A procession of scouts, school children and other Biddulph societies making their way to the Grange on 12 June 1924 on the occasion of the hospital's official opening.

Biddulph War Memorial to the men who died in the First World War being unveiled in May 1922 by Corporal J. Gibson, late of the Grenadier Guards. It was erected by Jonah Cotterill of Biddulph. The memorial is of grey Aberdeen granite set on a Kerridge sandstone base and the figure is of Cararra marble.

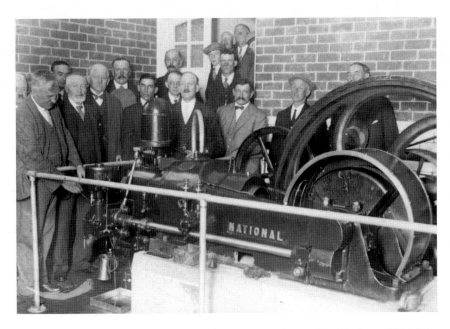

Cllr G. Lawton turning on the water at the new pumping station, Elmhurst, Biddulph, on 4 July 1929. The water was drawn from a borehole drilled down to the underlying millstone grit sandstone.

A 1948 children's Christmas party, held in the now demolished Biddulph Prize Band Club in Tunstall Road.

Opposite above: A stone-laying ceremony at the Miners Welfare Institute in New Street, Biddulph Moor, *c.* 1930. On 29 September 1951 it became the Sunday School for the Hill Top Methodist Church.

Opposite below: Mr Albert Sutton, Chairman of the Biddulph Urban District Council, placing an initialled brick at the building of the Biddulph Moor New Street Welfare Club.

The first Biddulph Carnival, held in 1965, was organised in aid of the Biddulph Swimming Bath Fund. Here it is seen passing through the lower High Street on its way to Cote Ground Farm where the swimming baths were later to be built. A parade of floats and traction engines stretched for half a mile and thousands of people lined the route, 5,000 of whom later joined in the competitions and revelries on the proposed site. (*Congleton/Biddulph Chronicle*)

Children were among the first bathers when the £133,000 Biddulph swimming pool was opened in June 1973. £45,000 of its cost was raised over the previous eight years from carnivals, sponsored walks and many other fundraising activities. (*Congleton/Biddulph Chronicle*)

nine

Societies

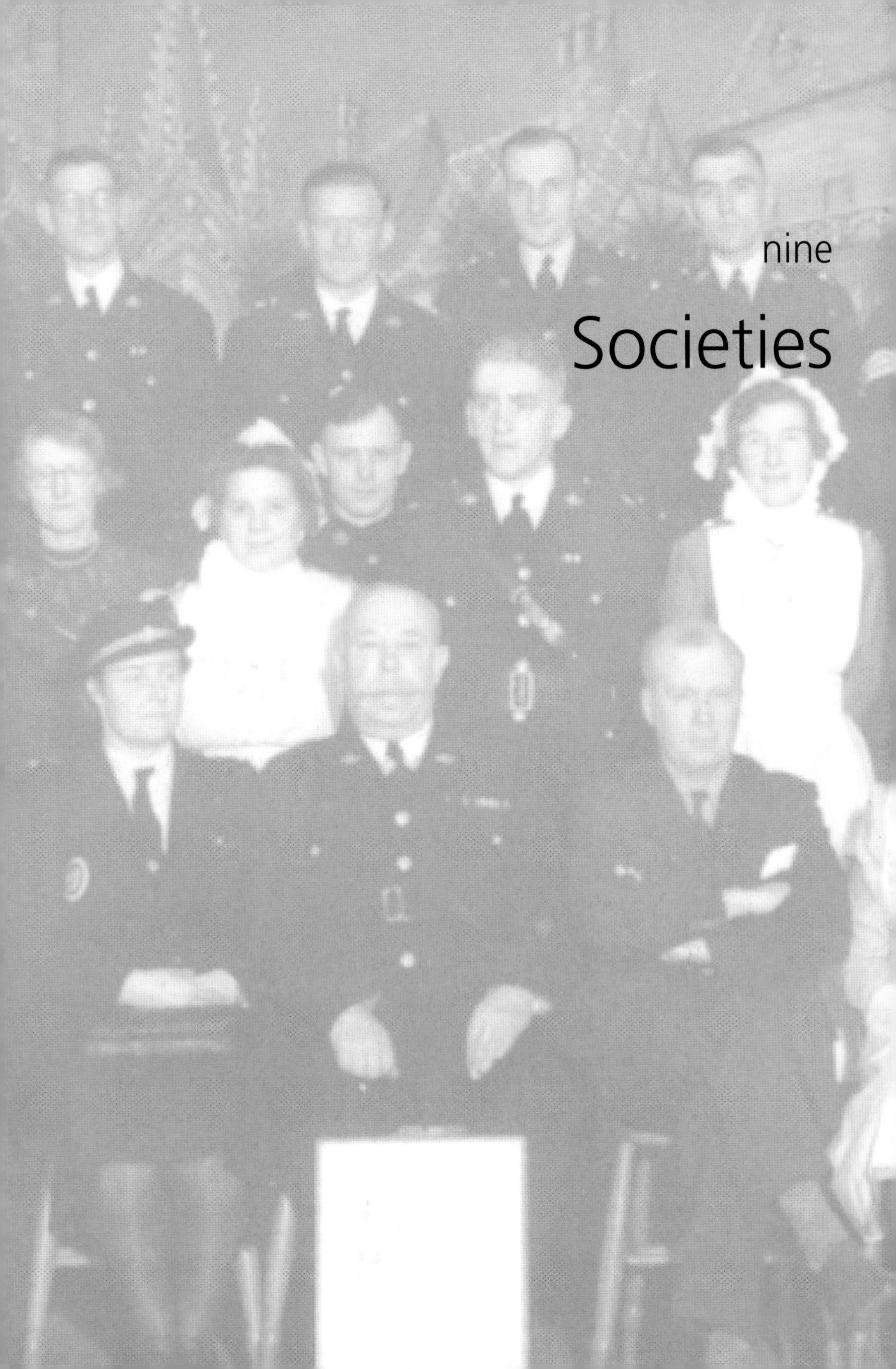

The Biddulph Company of Girl Guides standing in front of the gymnasium built in Wharf Road in 1909. The gentleman in the top hat is Mr Albert Sutton, who was chairman of Biddulph Urban District Council from 1925 to 1928.

Opposite Above: Wesleyan Methodist Men's Society. From left to right, back row: Mr Donald Nixon, -?- , Mr William Kirkham, Mr Ernest Sanderson, Mr Arthur Morris, Mr Jack Whitehurst. Middle row: Mr Horace Moss, Mr Frederick Downes, Mr Jack Poole, Mr Sydney Powell, Mr Frank Gibson, Mr George Clowes, Mr Leonard Kirkham, Mr Leonard Higginson, Mr Jack Hancock. Front row: Mr Albert Whitehurst, Mr Dennis Nixon, Mr Walter Hancock, Mr Harold Nixon, Mr William Bibby, Mr Edward Poole, Mr Leonard Ash.

Opposite below: A visit made by the Staffordshire branch of the National Farmers Union on 11 August 1932 to Port Sunlight. From left to right, front row: third is Mr Alfred Clowes, fifth Mr Thomas Warren, seventh Mr Hugh Kirkham, eighth Mr Arthur Heathcote. Second row: first Mr Ernest House, third Mr James Sargeant, sixth Mr Ambrose Rowbottom, seventh Mr Arthur Meakin, NFU secretary, eighth Mr Daniel Bostock, ninth Mr James Machin. At the extreme rear is Mr John Bailey.

St John's Ambulance officials. From left to right, middle row: first Mr Smith Holmes, eighth the wife of Jabez Oakes, a Biddulph chemist, ninth Mr G.L. Kay, clerk to Biddulph Council. Front row: second Mrs Biddulph, fifth Mr Herbert Chesterton, sixth Dr John Murphy, seventh Mrs Ferguson.

St John's Ambulance Brigade nurses (Biddulph branch), *c.* 1945. From left to right, back row: Mrs Zena Maydew, Mrs M. Pratt, Mrs E. Walley, Mrs Nessie Casstles, Mrs May Archer. Third row: Mrs D. Higgins, Mrs G. Brandreth, Mrs Barker, -?-, Mrs Sutton, Mrs Phyllis Copeland, Mrs Josephine Fricker, Mrs Margaret Bradbury. Second row: Mrs Doris Sutton, Mrs Phyllis Barlow, -?-, Mrs Forster, Mrs Agnes Holmes, -?-, Mrs Lawton, Mrs Margaret Leadbeater. Front row: Mrs Jepson, Mrs Charlesworth, Mrs Ferguson (wife of Dr Ferguson), Mrs Biddulph (wife of Mr R. Biddulph, headmaster), Mrs Mabel Moss, Mrs N. Bradbury.

Biddulph Nursing Association, 1939/45. Back row centre: Mrs Mildred Stoddard. Middle row, third from left: Mrs Madge Sherratt. Front row, from left: second Mrs Charles worth, sixth Mrs Morten, seventh Mrs A. Jepson, tenth Mrs Doris Hancock.

Biddulph Nursing Association taking part in a procession through Biddulph, being led by Mrs Morton.

Air-raid wardens recruited from within Cowlishaw Walkers workforce to deal with any fires which may have been caused by incendiary bombs dropped by the Germans during the Second World War. From left to right, back row: Mr Frederick Ogden, Mr Grimwood, Mr Noel Clark, Mr Stanley Morris, Mr Alex Hilton, Mr Charles Clark, –?–, Mr Joseph Lovatt, Mr Leslie Higgs, Mr Kelly, Mr Norman Rodgers, Mr Jack Hancock, Mr Frederick Cooke, Mr William Cooke and Mr Victor Sanders. Front row: Mr Moses Proctor, Mr Daniel Lawton, Mr Robert Petrie (works manager), Mr Horace Doorbar, Mr Edward Ogden and Mr Victor Sanders.

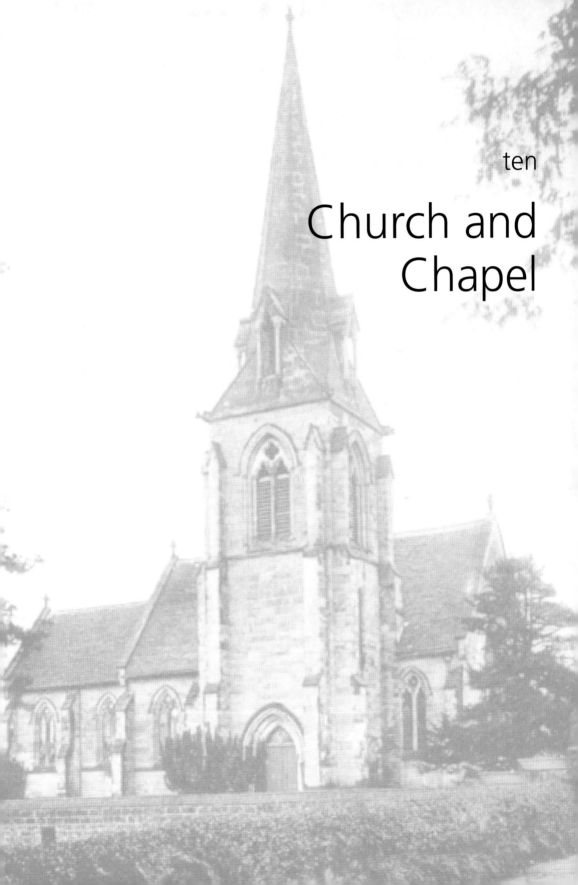

ten

Church and
Chapel

The A527 Tunstall to Congleton road passing Biddulph parish church of St Lawrence, on which site a church has stood from at least the twelfth century. Before the 1820 turnpike road to Congleton was constructed along the line of the present A527, the 1770 turnpike road from Tunstall to Bosley ran on the east side of the church, passing the Talbot Inn to cross the Leek to Congleton turnpike road close to Overton.

Spring Grove is shown on the 1876 first edition Ordnance Survey map as a vicarage and was probably built in 1874 at the same time as St Lawrence Church School. This was the same time that Robert Heath moved into the Grange, closing the road running to the east of the church and replacing it with the present Grange Road. In 1884 Mr John Venables was living in the house. In the 1901 census he was eighty-two years of age and described as a retired farmer; he was still living there in 1907. In 1928, and perhaps sometime before, Frederick Pointon of the adjacent nurseries was resident there.

Right: The splendid Alter Tomb in St Lawrence church, erected in 1655 in memory of Sir William Bowyer and now to be found in the north-west corner of the church. It was originally sited on the south side of the chancel, where Sir William and his wife were buried. The tomb was moved to its present site when the Heath chapel was created at the eastern end of the south isle in memory of the eldest son, William (aged twenty-five), and the eldest daughter, Mary (aged twenty-eight), of Robert and Ann Heath, who both died in 1872.

Left: The Norman font in St Lawrence church on its original site at the western end of the church beneath the tower. The tower, which was rebuilt in the early sixteenth century on the foundations of an earlier one, remained unaltered when the rest of the church was rebuilt in the 1830s.

The south aspect of St Lawrence vicarage, Biddulph. It was built in 1874, together with the Church School, when Robert Heath took up residence at the Grange. Prior to this, there was no vicarage house for the Biddulph parish. In the seventeenth century the ancient Grange Farm was owned by the Bowyer family, one of whom was the vicar of Biddulph parish and resided in the Grange house. Thus the house and surrounding land became known as the Vicarage estate. It was bought by John Bateman in 1812 and from 1831 to 1841 his wife's brother, the Revd William Henry Holt, lived there until James Bateman took up residence, his uncle moving to the newly built house called Elmhurst.

Looking towards St Lawrence church and vicarage from the east. The gentleman on the left is the Revd David Brodie, who was the vicar from 1892 to 1906. A maidservant can be seen looking out from an upstairs bedroom window.

Biddulph North School's first Rose Queen at Biddulph St Lawrence vicarage, June 1953. From left to right, back row: Sybil Davies, David Moss, David Mayer, Edward Linney, Angus Cunningham, Graham Haydon. Middle row: Alan Crudgington, Kathleen Hartshorn, Diane Moss, Miriam Clowes, Jose Jolliffe, Christine Plant (Queen), Susan Breeze, Jean Goodwin, Phyllis Burton, Roger Casstles. Front row: Peter Nixon, Robert Marsh, Daphne Grudgington, Anne Dobson, Carol Oakes, Pauline Brown, Sheila Dobson, Christine Potts, Leslie Poole, John Smith.

Biddulph North School, 1955. The Rose Queen with her father and mother, William and Vera Goodwin. The attendants, from left to right, back row, are: Sheila Dobson, Ann Dobson, Kathleen Hartshorne, Beryl Marsh. Front row: Isobel Holmes, Christine Mayer, Joan Whalley, Daphe Crudgington (Queen), Jean Goodwin, Audrey Brown, Pauline Brown, Christine Bailey, Marion Clowes.

Biddulph North School Rose Queen, 1956. From left to right, back row: Roger Bailey, Margaret Peet, retiring Queen Jean Goodwin, Kenneth Atherton, Roger Casstles, Stephen Bond, Kenneth Walters. Front row: Margaret Wilbraham, Margaret Brough, Pauline Nixon, Vivienne Carp, Elizabeth Leese, Miriam Clowes (Queen), John Fynney, John Wood, Donald Moss, Peter Price, Sheila Goodwin, Linda Homer. Kneeling: Ian Bridgett.

Knypersley church seen from the east. Built as a private church in 1850 by John Bateman of Knypersley Hall, it was not until 1922 that the parish of Knypersley was created, the church consecrated and the Revd C.A. Wood (previously its curate) installed as the first vicar. Behind the church and on the opposite side of the road is the original parsonage, which was later enlarged to become the home of Robert Heath's general manager, Mr Bruce Harding.

Left: The north side of Knypersley church as seen from Tunstall Road. The church and schoolhouse were built at a cost of £10,000 by John Bateman of Knypersley Hall. It was designed in the Early English style by Edward Cooke (who designed many of the features in James Bateman's Grange garden) and consists of a chancel, nave, south transept and tower on the north-west side containing one bell.

Below: Biddulph Moor Christ Church choir in 1915. The Revd Edwin Wheeldon of St Bees was installed as the rector in 1905, the living being in the gift of Robert Heath Esq.

The demolition of the Central Methodist chapel in January 1980 to make way for a new building. Built in 1880 as the Primitive Methodist chapel and one of the three chapels in Biddulph town, it became the centre of the amalgamated Primitive and Wesleyan Methodist Church. (*Congleton /Biddulph Chronicle*)

Opposite above: Station Road Methodist Women's Bright Hour outside The Manse, Halls Road, in 1919. Back row centre: Mrs Adshead. Third row: third from left, Mrs Powell, second from right, Mrs Lillie Moss. Second row: second from left, Mrs Hilda Bridgett with her daughter Flora on her knee, third from left is Mrs Baddiley with her daughter Olive. Front row: first Harry Bridgett, third Jack Gibson, fourth Harry Gibson.

Opposite below: Station Road, Biddulph, formerly Chapel Street, was renamed in 1896 by the new Urban District Council, which had been created in December 1894 to succeed the old Parish Council. The first Primitive Methodist chapel built in Biddulph in 1880 is on the right. Now called the Central Methodist chapel, it has been replaced by a new building on the same site. There is now a plan to demolish what was once the old school and replace it with a modern hall.

Brown Lees church members, *c.* 1945. In the photograph are Mrs T. Bennison, Mrs W.T. Archer, Mrs H. Bailey, Mrs E. Brough, Mrs Williams, Mrs C. Reynolds, Mary Sutton, Mrs Brookes, Mrs Edwards, Mrs Wooliscroft, Mrs Tooth, Mr Wilfred Archer, Miss Sutton, Mrs G. Duckworth, Mrs A. Ball, Mr Cyril Reynolds, Mr Lingham, Mr T. Bennison, Mr A. Gibson, Mr White, Mr A. Sutton, Mrs Reynolds, Mr E. Archer, Mrs E. Archer, Mrs S. Reynolds and Mrs Lingham.

Opposite above: Brown Lees Methodist choir, *c.* 1930.

Opposite below: Childerplay Mothers Union, *c.* 1920. Built by Robert Heath in 1880 for the workers of his nearby Biddulph Valley Coal & Ironworks, it was known locally as Heath's Mission. It sported a very successful football team, the players having to be a member of the bible class. The ladies are, from left to right, back row: Mrs Moreton, Mrs Ruth Grindley, Mrs Street, Polly Bowyer, Mrs Turner, Mrs Round, Mrs Bates, Mrs Hulme, Tilly Winkle, –?–. Front row: Mrs Winkle, Mrs Farmer, Mrs Mitchell, Mrs Lawton, Mr Hamlett (Minister), Mrs Hamlett, Mrs Humphies, Mrs Caddy, Mrs Wilson.

Other local titles published by Tempus

Biddulph
DEREK J. WHEELHOUSE

Once an isolated, infertile but beautiful region dominated by moorland, ridges and hills such as Mow Cop, it was not until the Industrial Revolution that the Biddulph Valley, with its valuable rock strata and the arrival of the railway, became a focal point for industry and population. Derek J. Wheelhouse has used his extensive local knowledge to produce this evocative collection of vivid images that will both charm and captivate all Bidolfians.
0 7524 1017 2

Congleton History & Guide
JOAN P. ALCOCK

Many Congleton residents will know the story of how the townspeople sold their Bible in the seventeenth century in order to buy a new bear, but details of other episodes from the town's history may be less well known. This engaging study, illustrated with over 100 photographs and a variety of other archive material, presents for the first time a chronological history of this Cheshire market town, from Neolithic times to the twenty-first century.
0 7524 2946 9

Newcastle under Lyme
DELYTH ENTICOTT AND NEIL COLLINGWOOD

Located at the confluence of several major road transport routes, Newcastle developed as a town following the strategic siting of a castle there in the twelfth century. A large produce market was established outside the castle and, because of this, Newcastle became for centuries the most important town in the area. This fascinating collection of over 200 photographs explores the historic borough of Newcastle under Lyme, covering not only the urban history of the borough but also the everyday aspects of life in its rural districts.
0 7524 2074 7

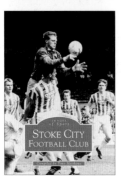

Stoke City Football Club
TONY MATTHEWS

As founder members of the Football League, Stoke City FC has a long and proud tradition. This book illustrates their impressive history with over 200 images, including old team groups, action shots, player portraits and programme covers, each supported by a detailed caption from the football statistician and experienced sports writer, Tony Matthews. Included in the selection are pictures featuring various promotion seasons, cup runs and other significant events sure to appeal to older fans and youger supporters interested in this club's fine sporting heritage.
0 7524 1698 7

If you are interested in purchasing other books published by Tempus, or in case you have difficulty finding any Tempus books in your local bookshop, you can also place orders directly through our website

www.tempus-publishing.com